Edward Bouverie Pusey

Un-science, not Science, adverse to Faith

A Sermon preached before the University of Oxford. Second Edition

Edward Bouverie Pusey

Un-science, not Science, adverse to Faith
A Sermon preached before the University of Oxford. Second Edition

ISBN/EAN: 9783337115814

Printed in Europe, USA, Canada, Australia, Japan

Cover: Foto ©ninafisch / pixelio.de

More available books at **www.hansebooks.com**

UN-SCIENCE, NOT SCIENCE, ADVERSE TO FAITH.

A SERMON

PREACHED BEFORE THE UNIVERSITY OF OXFORD

ON

THE TWENTIETH SUNDAY AFTER TRINITY, 1878.

BY THE

REV. E. B. PUSEY, D.D.

REGIUS PROFESSOR OF HEBREW, AND CANON OF CHRIST CHURCH.

SECOND EDITION.

SOLD BY

JAMES PARKER & CO., OXFORD

AND 377, STRAND, LONDON;

AND RIVINGTONS

LONDON, OXFORD, AND CAMBRIDGE.

1878.

A SERMON [a].

S. John i. 27.

*" There standeth One among you, Whom ye
know not."*

WHY is the study of the physical sciences at this
time so often adverse to the faith in God, and His
Son, Jesus Christ our Lord? There is no doubt alas !
that it is so : the long list of eminent scientific men
of old, of unimpaired faith, shews that it need not be
so. To consider why of late it has been so, may, by
God's blessing, save individuals from being borne
away into the whirlpool.

It is not that the book of God's works contradicts
the book of God's Word, or even that man's inter-
pretation of the one book contradicts his interpreta-
tion of the other. They move in two different
spheres, and cross each other's path only in the most
elementary points. The sphere of the Bible is the
revelation which God makes of Himself to man, what
He has declared of Himself, of His Being, His Attributes, His relation to His creatures and of His
creatures to Him; what duties that revelation im-
poses upon man; how man may correspond to the
purposes of that revelation; why he failed; how he

[a] The writer, having the opinion of an eminent physician that
this sermon was too long for his powers of delivery, and not
knowing how to shorten it, the sermon was actually delivered by
his friend the Rev. H. P. Liddon, D.D.

A

may recover; what God has done to restore him,
nay to raise him above his original creation in grace:
how He daily helps him in his struggle with sin, on
his way, step by step, upwards to Himself; how he
may attain to the end, for which he was created, likeness to God, love of God, union with God, attaining
to God, the blessed-making sight of God, in all eternity; and, on God's side, by what rule of His ever-
lasting justice holiness and mercy, He will, after
this life, dispose of each individual soul whom He
has made and has redeemed. The sphere of physical
science is the material.

The basis of a lasting peace and alliance between
physical science and Theology is, that neither should
intrude into the province of the other. This is also
true science. For science is *certain* knowledge based
on *certain* facts. The facts on which Theology rests
are spiritual facts; those of physical science are
material.

Theology has wisely gone back to the wisdom of
S. Augustine, who deprecated a Christian's supporting opinions on physical science by the authority of
Holy Scripture[b]. "When they [the better-instructed
heathen]" says this father, "discover some Christian in error in a matter which they themselves know
thoroughly, and supporting his opinion out of our
books, how are they to believe those books on the
resurrection of the dead, the hope of life eternal, and
the kingdom of heaven, when they think them written delusively on things which they can know by
actual experience or certain calculations? It cannot
be said, what anxiety and sorrow these rash dogma-

b S. Aug. de Gen. ad lit. i. 39.

tisers inflict on their wiser brethren, if, when they
are blamed and convicted of the rashness and false-
hood of their opinion by those who are not bound
by the authority of our books, they endeavour to
defend, what they have said with most inconsiderate
rashness or most evident error, out of the same sacred
books, without understanding either what they say
or whereof they affirm."

Peter Lombard sums up the mind of those before
him. " ᶜ Man, by sinning, lost not the knowledge [of
natural things,] nor how to provide things necessary
to his being. And therefore in Scripture man is not
instructed in these things, but in the knowledge of
the soul which by sinning he had lost."

Theology is even bound, not to lay down as certain truth any one meaning of Holy Scripture, when-
ever its words are any how capable of another. Again
says the same thoughtful father, who had struggled
through wild error to the light of truth, " ᵈ If in
things obscure and far removed from our sight, we
read anything even in Divine Scripture, which may,
without injury to the faith wherewith we are em-
bued, yield different meanings, let us not, by any
hasty affirmations, so precipitate ourselves into any
one of them, that, if a more diligent discussion of the
truth should really shake it, we should fall with it,
contending, not for the mind of the Divine Scriptures
but for our own, so as to wish that Holy Scripture
should mean what we mean, whereas we ought to
wish the meaning of the Scripture to be our's."

True Theology then precipitates nothing. It has
no preconceived opinions in a province which is not

ᶜ L. ii. Dist. 23.   ᵈ S. Aug. de Gen. ad lit. i. 37.

its own. It cannot accept as certain truth, unproved guesses, imaginations as to what might be in God's Omnipotence, but cannot be proved ever to have been ; it cannot accept alleged want of proof that a thing is, to be a proof that it is not. On the solid foundation of the Rock, whereon it stands, it looks out securely on the conflict of human opinions, as they toss to and fro on the salt and bitter sea of this tempestuous world. It looks out securely, but with pity; thankful for its own security, anxious that others, who now, amid their wanderings, seek the same path of life, yet seek it not where it is to be found, should also find it ; jealous over itself that it repel them not, by questioning anything, which, although as yet unproved, at least contradicts not the higher truths, of which it is the constituted guardian, lest perchance there should be a basis of truth, which should ultimately emerge out of the chaos, on which the Spirit of God has not yet brooded.

. Geology has increased its demands. It fills up time with its periods, and its periods as it wills ; it goes back from transformation to transformation, as far as imagination can reach along its millions of years, until the earth be but a formless mass of independent atoms (as it imagines), floating in ether. Theology accompanies it, undisturbed, (since time is no measure for eternity,) and when it has reached its utmost bound, and imagination is lost and dizzied in that all-but-endless time, repeats calmly the words of Moses, " In the beginning God created the heaven and the earth." The words of Moses remain a truth, which theorisers may keep out of sight, but have no grounds of science to deny. Even to human science it at least remains probable, that an effect implies a cause.

Yet although Theology looks on the question of time as outside of its own teaching, it would be well for Geology to come to a result within itself, before it turns its results against revelation. Time, it has been said, costs nothing to Geologists. "Truly," said one who once taught here, "it does not." Else, I may add, they would not be so spendthrift of it. But neither does it to Almighty God. It has not indeed the precision which we might expect of an exact science, when one writer[e] demands 353 millions of years for the formation of the solid basis of the earth. A calculation, whose units are millions, has an apparent, rather than a real exactness. Yet Theology says to it, 'do as you will: it concerns not me : theology is concerned only with the religious aspect of creation, how God, Who created all things, placed man in his trial-time upon this earth. With any pre-historic period I have nothing to do : I will receive whatever you establish, but I cannot receive these conjectures as matters of faith :' 'I will welcome the most romantic imaginations of science, if only science will not erect them into articles of faith against the faith.' Conjectures have often led to the discovery of truth ; but until any truth is discovered, they lie outside of science. In science too we must teach as truth only what we *know*.

Of the formation of the earth Theology would equally admit of Lucretius' combination of atoms floating in space, and drawn together by mutual at-

[e] G. Bischoff quoted by Caussette, Le bon sens de la foi ii. 405.
[f] Caussette Ib. 389.

traction, provided only that He Who gave them those impulses, and placed each individual at the distances, whence that attraction would act, was—not chance, but God.

To Theology creation is equally magnificent, whether the earth started into existence at once at the command of God, when "[g]the angels shouted for joy" at the formation of this our scene of trial, where we should be fitted to be as they; or whether God created matter, in countless molecules, to be attracted together through a property which He imparted to them, each and all. Theology looks with equal impartiality on all geological theories, "[h]atomism, plutonism, neptunism, convulsionism, quietism," provided that, in whatever way it pleased our Creator to act, this be laid at the foundation, that the earth was not eternal, but was created; and that it was at His will, that it passed through whatever transformations it underwent, in conformity to the laws which He imposed upon it.

To Theology all explanations of the details of the six days of creation are indifferent. The mission of Moses was to announce a Creator to a benighted world, and that man was the work of God's hands, formed in His own likeness, having the stamp of His own Divinity upon him, receiving his life and soul immediately from Himself. In what sense the word "day" is to be explained; whether Moses speaks of six periods of 24 hours, or of unlimited periods; whether those periods were closely consecutive on one another; whether the sun broke through a dense vapour enveloping the earth, on that glorious dawn

[g] Job xxxviii. 7. [h] Caussette Ib. 402.

of the fourth day, having been before hidden from it, and the moon and the stars then first shone upon the earth in its evening; whether even the works of the Hexaemeron took place in the order, in which they are related; where comes in all that history, which the recent study of the catacombs of the earth un- folds, whether in the six days or periods, or before them; whether Moses is relating the renewal of the face of the earth, after some sentence passed upon its former inhabitants,—on all this and more, genuine Theology says nothing, and is even jealous over her- self, lest she should seem to invest any physical theory with the sacredness of Divine truth.

It ranked formerly among objections to the reve- lation by Moses, that he recorded the creation of light before that of the sun. Now that it is known that light is independent of the sun's orb, Theology abstains from ascribing to Moses astronomical know- ledge, nor will it claim for him geological, on account of some seeming correspondence between the work of the six days and the layers discovered by geology. Theology has been taught, Who gave being to all which has being. If human speculation or research thinks that it can discover in what order God created, Theology leaves it to decipher God's book of nature as it can; whatsoever it may establish as certain truth, it is ready to receive as a human supplement to its Divine knowledge; but possibilities, conjectures, however they may lead to truth, are not yet ascer- tained truth.

So as to the miracle of Joshua[i], it has even been

[i] See Lap. on Ecclus. xlvi. 5. p. 954. See also Reusch, Bibel und Natur, pp. 25, 26. ed. 1876.

a common opinion, that Holy Scripture does not lay
down, how the light was prolonged, and that Joshua
spoke only, as any astronomer of this day would,
when he says, The sun "rises," The sun "sets."
The question belongs to that of miracles, as a supernatural order of things, not to the relation of this
particular miracle to physical science.

Our Lord, as well as Moses, tells us that the deluge
was universal as to man all but the eight persons
in the ark : Moses tells us nothing about the earth,
because it does not concern us. One expression of
Moses is obviously metaphoric. He says nothing
about the means, natural or supernatural, whereby
it was brought about. "The fountains of the great
deep" might have been equally " broken up," whether, it pleased God to use volcanic agency, or the
waters of the deep[j]. Natural science then has nothing to oppose, because nothing is said. Moses
only tells us that God foretold what He would do,
and that those who neglected His warning perished,
as it will be, our Lord tells us, at the end.

   Physical science at one time believed, perhaps
some still believe, in spontaneous generation : no
one ever saw an instance of it : but the naturalist contradicts it, not the theologian. Scientific knowledge
denies it; Theology would be willing to receive it,
if it were proved. Theology places no limits on the

  [j] See at length, Reusch, Bibel und Natur, pp. 289—318. He
quotes Pianciani, a Jesuit father, Cosmogonia p. 519. 'Moses
mentions neither volcanoes, nor elevations of chains of mountains,
nor sinkings of the level of the earth, nor any other phenomena,
which could either precede or accompany or follow the Flood :
but neither does he exclude any of these or other phenomena, and
so one can admit them without contradicting his testimony.'

modes of *His* working, Who works all things in all.
If God willed that organic life should start out of inorganic masses, Theology would accept it at once,
since our Lord has said, "[k] My Father worketh hitherto and I work." It would be to Theology only a renewal of what it already believes, that "[l] God formed
man of the dust of the ground and breathed into his
nostrils the breath of life, and man became a living
soul." The workings in nature are to Theology only
the workings of God. For nature, although men
ascribe to it wisdom and power, and personify it as if
it were a goddess, is but a name for an effect, whose
Cause is God. But science too says, "[m] Tertium non
datur. There is no other choice left; either spontaneous generation, or a Creator. If any lay down,'I
accept not creation;' then his second thesis must be,
'Then I accept spontaneous generation.' But for
this we have no evidence of fact."

Again, physical science now assumes as certain
truth (would that it believed truths of the Word of
God as unhesitatingly!) an unproved theory, that
Almighty God did not create all the forms of animal creation at once, but some primordial germs
only, out of which all the rest were evolved. Evolution is, for the day, a sort of Gospel, or at least
an axiom of physical science. Apart from unproved
and unprovable and therefore unscientific details, the
principle, that God *may* have created some things in
that "[n] of all things which have their birth corpor-

---

[k] S. John v. 17.   [l] Gen. ii. 7.

[m] Virchow, Die Freiheit der Wissenschaft, p. 20.

[n] de Trin. iii. 8. n. 13. See other passages in Mivart's ' Origin of
Species,' pp. 304, 305. Dublin Review Vol. xvii. N.S. pp. 8—16.

eally and visibly, some hidden seeds lie hid in those
corporeal elements of this world," is no other than the
teaching of our Western Theology since S. Augustine.
Far more developement might be granted, than science can prove, a wider range might be given to the
popular theory of evolution than exact science yet
admits of ; the number of species of which human experience knows, might be reduced indefinitely, without contradicting the Bible history of the creation;
" °God made the beast of the earth after his kind, and
cattle after their kind, and every thing that creepeth
upon the earth, after his kind."
To our unimaginative minds, the unity of types
in creation, amid a variety which the human mind
cannot grasp, seems more explicable by the unity of
its Author than by transformist theories. Even in
works of human creativeness (as works of art, fiction,
poetry, even music) we are accustomed to recognise
sameness of authorship by some recurring characte-
ristic. We do not ascribe it to poverty of imagination, but to some pleasure which the soul takes in
its creations. But while we think the transformist
theories a mere imagination, Theology does not hold
them excluded by Holy Scripture, so that they spare
the soul of man P.
Theology then gives to natural science the knowledge of God : it does not interfere with itself.
Some of the adherents of natural science seem even

° Gen. i. 25.

P "The position of faith with regard to the theories of evolution seems to be this. It is not contrary to faith, that all living
things *up to man exclusively* were evolved by natural law out of
minute life-germs primarily created, or even out of inorganic
matter." Dublin Review. Ib. p. 38.

impatient with Theology, that Theology will not contradict it, that so science might have an excuse to reject it.

"Negative Atheism," says one [q] speaking for natural science, "is the outcome of science." Why so? It was not so formerly. "[r] The heavens," David bursts forth, "evermore declare the glory of God, and the firmament sheweth His handy-work. Day unto day poureth forth speech, and night unto night sheweth knowledge." It is one universal language, understood without utterance. They speak, because they are. "There is no speech, no words; their voice is not heard: their line is gone out through all the earth and their words to the end of the world." Why are they silent to any now? Why is their mute speech no longer understood? What has dulled the inner ear? The glory of the nightly heavens made David marvel at God's great condescension to man [s]. They have the same wondrous piercing transporting beauty now. Why to one class of minds do they give rise to speculations only, out of what nebulæ they were condensed, or to another furnish arguments that God would not have regard to the inhabitants of a world so small as ours? As if the geographic extent of a world were the measure of its intrinsic value, and God were bound by a law of necessity, not to shew forth the greatest marvels of His condescension to the very lowest of His rational creation; or as if S. Paul were necessarily wrong when he spoke of the design of God, that "[t] now unto the

---

[q] Drysdale, 'Is scientific materialism compatible with dogmatic Theology?' p. 53.　　　　[r] Ps. xix. 1-6.

[s] Ps. viii.　　　　[t] Eph. iii. 10.

principalities and powers in heavenly places might
be known through the Church the manifold wisdom
of God;" or that the Apostles, in their conflict with
the world which would destroy them, were "ᵘa
spectacle unto the world *and to angels* and to men;"
or S. Peter, that "ˣ *angels* desire to stoop down and
look into" the mysteries of our salvation.

Whether any of those heavenly hosts, of which
Theology knows, dwell locally in other worlds;
whether, although unadapted to the existence of beings of the like physical condition with ourselves,
God has peopled them with inhabitants fitted to exist
in them, Theology leaves to His Infinite Wisdom. It
has not pleased God to reveal it to us here, because
it does not concern us to know. To us too it seems
most probable, that that brilliant, but inanimate, creation is somehow full of intelligent life; and if so, then
it is full of fellow-citizens of ours, children of the same
God although not of the same race; severed in those
almost measureless spaces, but joined with us in our
adoration of the God of all, and uttering with us
the Angelic hymn, " Holy, Holy, Holy, Lord God of
Sabaoth : Heaven and earth are full of Thy glory."
The unknown and unrevealed can be no argument
against that which is known, because revealed.
Pseudo-science declares that "ʸ to the really pious
man, the thought that all which lives is allied to
him is an instruction full of interest." Theology
teaches us that our fellow-citizenship is not with the
brutes, but with the angels, to whom, our Lord tells

ᵘ 1 Cor. iv. 9.   ˣ 1 S. Pet. i. 12.
ʸ " He who reflects not will find therein matter for laughter;
but the man who is truly pious &c." C. Vogt in Caussette ii. 537.

us, they who shall be "ᶻaccounted worthy to obtain that world," "shall be equal."

[David again speaks of the developement in his mother's womb, almost, but for his reverence, as if he were writing in our century. "ᵃ*Thou* hast created my inward parts; Thou didst interweave ᵇ me [with nerves and veins and arteries] in my mother's womb: my substance ᶜ (his self, his undeve-. loped substance) was not hid from Thee, when I was made in secret, and variegated ᵈ (with all the intricacy of our physical structure.) Thine eyes did see my formless substance ᵉ; the ball, which was afterwards to be unwound, as what lay yet undeve-. loped was expanded into the rudimental shape of the future being: "and in Thy book were they all written ᶠ, which day by day were formed, when as yet there were none of them." But that Theology would not identify David's words with modern physical theories, we might speak of this as a doctrine of the evolution of the individual. Yet David believed in his Maker and glorified Him. His own creation was to him matter of awe and admiration and praise.

S. Paul tells us that "ᵍthe invisible things of God from the creation of the world are clearly seen, being understood by the things that are made, even His eternal power and Godhead, so that they are without excuse." Much modern science says, that they not only had excuse, but that they were right; for that the things made give no witness to their Maker.]

ᶻ S. Luke xx. 35.   ᵃ Ps. cxxxix. 13.

ᵇ חסכני   ᶜ עצמי   ᵈ רקמתי   ᵉ גלמי

ᶠ I prefer the E. V. It is natural to use יצר of the framing of the human frame, not of the days of human life.

ᵍ Rom. i. 20.

B

Since then Theology restrains itself within its own bounds, keeps itself clear of Physical Science, and accepts every certain conclusion of Physical Science, as man's unfolding of God's book of nature, why this unnatural relation of physical science to Theology? Why did, not David only, but Copernicus and Galileo, Newton and Kepler and Euler, look up and adore, and yet it has been said, in the name of modern science, "[h] The heavens no longer declare the glory of God, but that of La Place?" And yet nearly all the ideas of La Place on the origin of the globe have been accepted by a divine [i] who believes also in his God.

It may seem to be beginning a great way off, but, in a place of education, it is not amiss to say, 'One reason of this alienation of modern physical science, is its exclusiveness.' A thoughtful writer has said, "[j] Special studies, which bring into play a particular aptitude of intelligence, without paralysing the rest, are conformable to the wants of nature. Exclusive studies, which amass a sort of congestional life upon one point of the mind, leaving the rest in inaction, are an abnormal developement, an excrescence of intellectual life; so that while special science forms men who are eminent, exclusive science produces judgements which are false. Exclusive science is the only one injurious to religion; but it is also the only one opposed to it." "[k] What withholds a man from faith, is not the knowledge of nature, which

---

[h] quoted in Janet, Matérialisme contemp. en Allemagne. Caussette ii. 261.   [i] P. Pianciani in Caussette ii. 407.

[j] P. Caussette, Le bon sens de la foi. P. ii. L. iii. c. 1. T. ii. p. 233.

[k] Ib. p. 238.

any one has, but the knowledge of religion which he has not." We readily recognise in other subjects the special peril of exclusiveness, in narrowing the range of thought. Theological exclusiveness or narrowness is a by-word to physical science. Physicists would seem to hold it almost impossible, that a Theologian should not be narrow. It seems to them a strange phenomenon, a thing to be noted, when he is not so. Why, but because the all-importance of this study is supposed so to rivet the minds of those devoted to it as to indispose them to take in thoughts which lie outside of it, much more those which at first sight seem to impinge against it? It could hardly be held to be so universal a fruit of Theological study, unless there were some widely prevailing cause. It cannot be that the grandest study, in which wisdom power love goodness and all besides are infinite, should be narrowing, universally and alone. It must be a deep human infirmity, which should contract the conception of infinity. If the exclusive study of the highest be, as men say, narrowing, other studies may well look to it. This narrowing cannot be confined to Theology. It is not a mere retort, but the acknowledgement of a common human infirmity, if Theology says to Natural science, "Change but the name, the tale is told of thee."

"Any one study, of whatever kind, exclusively pursued," says a very thoughtful writer[1], "deadens in the mind the interest, nay the perception of any other. Thus Cicero says that Plato and Demosthenes, Aris-

[1] "Lectures on University subjects," by J. H. Newman, D.D. p. 322. 1859.

totle and Isocrates, might have respectively excelled
in each other's province, but that each was absorbed
in his own. His words are emphatic; 'each, delighted
with his own, *despised* the other's study.' Speci-
mens of this peculiarity occur every day. You can
hardly persuade some men to talk about anything but
their own pursuit; they refer the whole world to
their own centre, and measure all matters by their
own rule.—It is clear that the tendency of science
is to make men indifferentists or sceptics, merely by
being exclusively pursued."

And this it does, partly by losing sight of what is
spiritual, God, the soul, freewill, human responsibi-
lity, and all the truths of revelation, through being
immersed in the material; partly by forgetting the
bounds which belong to it *as science*, i.e. as accurate
knowledge, "ᵐ encroaching on territory not its own,
and undertaking problems which it has no instru-
ments to solve."

But, if physicists will bear with our saying it, exclusive study of natural science must be even more
liable to limit the range of vision than that of Theology. For Theology, if studied at all, necessitates
the study of a large range of subjects, connected with
the spiritual. Physical science has also a large
range, but it is wholly material. But matter and
spirit are not only separate; they are wholly distinct
from one another. To dwell exclusively upon the one
deadens the sense of the other. God, we know, is
wholly Spirit; we can form no sensible conception
of Him. We can know Him, love Him, adore Him;

ᵐ "Discourses on the scope and nature of University education," by J. H. Newman, D.D. p. 107. 1852.

we can feel His Presence, if He will; we may have
."a tingling sense of His Presence." Moses saw
Him Who is invisible. But we cannot imagine Him.
An idealist Philosopher disbelieved in the existence
of matter : much more easily may one who is con-
versant only with matter forget the existence of
spirit. "[n] The eye that looks too exclusively on
physical nature loses the habit of considering that
nature is not the whole of God's plan." A very
celebrated physical philosopher of this day says,
." [o] The *logical feebleness* of science is not sufficiently
borne in mind. It keeps down the weed of super-
stition, not by logic, but by slowly rendering the
mental soil unfit for its cultivation;" in other words,
"The mind, being bound down to what is material,
becomes unfit for the reception of spiritual truth,"
a verification of S. Paul's words, "[p] The natural man
understandeth not the things of the Spirit of God;
neither can he know them, because they are spiri-
tually discerned."

Modern science in England does not, for the most
part, *deny* God. Fanaticism, like that in Germany
which said, "[q] you must deny God and trample the
Cross under foot, before you can become even a scho-
lar, far less a master in Natural Science," would shock
in England by its coarse and naked blasphemy. But
science, which does not deny God, may *forget* Him.
It would very likely acknowledge Him, if it were
asked. But it is so busy about secondary causes,

[n] Dublin Review, Vol. xvii. N.S. Oct. 1871, p. 23.

[o] Prof. Tyndall, *Pall Mall Gazette* June 15. 1868.

[p] 1 Cor. ii. 14.

[q] Posner, Häkelogonie quoted by Dr. Drysdale, "Is scientific
materialism &c." p. 62.

that it has no time to think about the First Cause.
Time and thought are fully occupied without Him.
It goes back from link to link, and forgets that the
chain is but a weight, unless it is fastened some-
where. Every secondary cause is at once a cause and
an effect; an effect of what goes before, a cause of
what succeeds it. But where is the First Cause,
upon which it depends? Natural science has to do
with created things, how they act on each other.
The belief in a First Cause, or a Creator, belongs to
man, as a creature, not as an investigator of science.
It cannot find God or the soul at the bottom of its
crucible. This was the complaint of one very
eminent in science, "[r] I have sought God every
where, and have found Him no where." Why? but
because he sought Him, where he did not know how
to find Him, and sought Him not, where he might
have found Him, in Revelation or in his own soul.
The thought of a First Cause belongs to Theology,
or in its degree, to Philosophy, not to the natural
sciences. It is foreign to the researches of Physical
Science; so much so, that when one, who had traced
the developement of species through all links possible and impossible, closed his book, not as a philosopher but as a Theist, by speaking of life with its
several powers having "[s] been originally breathed by
the Creator into a few forms or into one," his expression was criticised, because it acknowledged God as
the Author of all. It, in fact, brings back the old

---

[r] Humboldt to the king of Prussia. Lalande is quoted as saying, "I have searched the heavens, but have no where found tho
traces of a God." Drysdale, "Is scientific materialism &c." p. 50.

[s] Darwin 'Origin of Species,' end.

belief, that God is the Ultimate Cause of all that is, because, at all events, He infused into those supposed primordial principles the power of generating, step by step, whatever was developed from them.

But there is an unconscious as well as a conscious disbelief in God; and the unconscious disbelief in Him is often the more dangerous, because the more subtle. To *deny* God, is more the sin of those rebellious spirits, who dispute His claim over our wills. To *forget* God may be human infirmity, in every thing which absorbs the mind, in intellectual ambition, as well as in the slavery to sense, or in the shadowy day-dreams of human greatness. "'Thy judgements," says David, "are far above out of his sight." They are above; he is below. Of the Holy One it is said, "ᵘ I have set God always before Me:" of the man of this world, "Thy judgements are high from before him." They do not come across him.

Yet to *deny* God requires more belief in God than to *forget* Him. To deny God implies that He has a claim to be believed; it virtually acknowledges the claim which it resists. God is in his thoughts, though as yet put away from them. The latent belief, though resisted and repelled, may, by God's mercy and grace, yet reassert itself, when the hindrance put to it by man's will is, by whatever means, withdrawn. The fast-closed doors may at length be opened. "I have known many of them," says Plato ˣ, "and can tell you this, that no one who had taken up in youth this opinion, that the gods do not exist, ever continued in the same till he was old."

ᵗ Ps. x. 5.　　　ᵘ Ib. xvi. 8.
ˣ Plato de Legg. l. x. p. 888. Vol. iv. p. 398. Jowett's Translation.

God has, as it were, slipped out of the memory of those who forget Him. He is to them a thing of the past. It may have more of contempt to forget Him. "So, brother," said a member of the Institute to a colleague [y], "decidedly God does not exist?" "He does *not* exist," was the answer; "modern science could not admit a hypothesis so absurd as God a Creator." "So you are quite certain?" was the reiterated question. "Perfectly certain." "[z] Well then, colleague, you are more credulous than I, for I know nothing about it."

Atheism has been formally pronounced to be "[a] a system too religious, because there is something better than to deny religion. It is to forget it."

Yet belief belongs to that perfection of man's nature, in which God created him. Something man must believe. "The time will come," says S. Paul[b] of times like these, " when they will not endure sound doctrine, and they shall turn away their ears from the truth, and shall be turned unto fables." "[c] I am come in My Father's Name," our Lord said to the Jews, "and ye believe Me not; another will come in his own name, and him ye will believe." All their history has verified His words. They rejected the true Christ. Not one false Christ has arisen since, whom, to their own temporal hurt also, they have not

---

[y] "One day M. Babinet came out of the palace of the Institute, with a colleague, a hardened mathematician, who eliminated God out of all his calculations, as an Unknown, irrational and disturbing. The two nihilists conversed freely. 'So, brother,' said M. Babinet, &c." quoted in Le bon sens de la foi ii. 314.

[z] "Eh bien, collègue," reprit M. Babinet avec son vaste sourire, &c." [a] Arnold Ruge, Annales de Halle, in Causette ii. 252.

[b] 2 Tim. iv. 3, 4.   [c] S. John v. 43.

received. "It is often and truly said," writes the rationalist historian of rationalism[d], "that past ages were preeminently credulous, as compared with our own; yet the difference is not so much in the amount of the credulity, as in the direction which it takes. Men are always prepared to accept on very slight evidence, what they believe to be exceedingly probable."

It belongs to that activity of mind, with which God endowed us, to long to know the cause of all causes. He *has* endowed us with the capacity of knowing the Cause of all causes, Himself. Only this is not the province of natural science. Atheistic science will own for itself, that it has nothing to do with the question. "A naturalist," one says[e], "can no more imagine the coming into existence of matter, than he can imagine its disappearance, and he therefore looks upon the existing quantity of matter in the universe as a given fact. If any person feels the necessity of conceiving the coming into existence of this matter, as the work of a supernatural creative power, of the creative force of something outside of matter, we have nothing to say against it.—Such a conception of an immaterial force, which at the first creates matter, is an article of faith, which has nothing whatever to do with human science. *Where faith commences, science ends.*" But then it is no longer *as* science, that it can call "science and faith" two "arts of the human mind[e]" or allege that faith "has its origin in the poetic imagination." The question has been very simply summed up[f]. "The physical

[d] Lecky i. 88.   [e] Haeckel's history of Creation T. i. 8, 9.

[f] Lectures and Essays on University Subjects by J. H. Newman, D.D. c. 6. 'Christianity and Physical Science,' pp. 228, 229.

philosopher has nothing whatever to do with final
causes, and will get into inextricable confusion, if he
introduces them into his investigations. He has to
look in one definite direction, not in any other.—
Within the limits of the phenomena and laws of the
material world he may speculate and prove; he may
trace the operation of the laws of matter through
periods of time; he may penetrate into the past, and
anticipate the future; he may recount the changes
which they have effected upon matter, and the rise,
growth, and decay of phenomena; and so in a certain sense he may write the history of the material
world, as far as he can; still he will always advance
from phenomena, and conclude, upon internal evidence which they supply. He will not come near the
questions, what that ultimate element is, which we
call matter; how it came to be; whether it can cease
to be; whether it ever was not; whether it will ever
come to nought; in what its laws really consist;
whether they can cease to be; whether they can be
suspended; what causation is; what time is; what
the relations of time to cause and effect, and a hundred other questions of a similar character."

The vast and wonderful progress of natural science
has tempted it, like so many other conquerors, to
over-pass its bounds. It goes beyond its bounds, if
it argues against creation, on the ground that the
emergence of matter into being is "ᵍ unthinkable;"
in other words, that we, being creatures of very
limited faculties, whose highest intelligence is the
capacity of conceiving an Intelligence infinitely
above our own, cannot think *how* that Intelligence

ᵍ Nineteenth Century, Sept. 1878. p. 445.

could act, or how It could effect what we cannot imagine, how It would effect.

But are then men so sure that they can form any idea of created things which they have every day in their mouths? What a puzzle are time and space, if we think of them in themselves, not of things which take place in them. "I find no difficulty in time or space," said Charles Lamb[h], "for—I never think about them." Time to come is a mere creature of the imagination; it is not yet, it may never be: time past has ceased to be. The present has no duration. Both exist only in the soul. Once time was not: there was nothing but God's ever-present eternity. Once again, we are told, it "[i] shall be no more." But even now, what is it? Time is present, only at this moment; in the next, what is now present, will have ceased to be. Time seems long or short, according to our own feelings. If we are weary, it seems to be long; if happy, short. It is not measured by the motion of the heavenly bodies or any other, but rather itself measures them; nor is it any measure of eternity. But what can we think of that, which has ceased to be in the single moment, in which we think of it? And yet it has such hold of our imagination, that we cannot picture to ourselves its not being.

Again we speak continually of "infinite space," but we are baffled and cast back upon ourselves, if we think of it: and at last the religious mind takes refuge in the thought, that it is the Presence of the Infinite God, Who is wholly every where, but the whole of Him no where.

[h] quoted Rambler, T ii. N. S. p. 362.
[i] Rev. x. 6. The difficulties as to time are mostly taken from S. Aug. Conf. xi. 10-31.

Even in mathematics we have things demonstrated
to us, which, if we attempt to set our demonstration
before our eyes, seem to us absolutely impossible [k].

What right then have we to reject anything because it is not "thinkable?"

But is it then more "thinkable," i. e. can we
better picture to ourselves, how a single "[l]cell of
protoplasm generated at the bottom of the sea"
should develope of itself into all this beautiful and
boundless variety of intricate forms every where
spread before our senses; or how "[m] vitality should
be generated out of matter," or how matter should
be self-existent, i. e. God; or how that "[n] God-
matter, in all eternity divided in thousands of millions of scattered atoms in imaginary spaces, should
once have been united by a law of arbitrary cohe-
sion, called chance?" Is not chance that God, to
escape the acknowledgment of Whose Being the
eternity of matter is assumed?

Again the action of the soul upon the body is pro-
scribed, because we know not how matter can act
upon spirit. Yet this too does not belong to physical
science. Physical science goes out of its domain, if it
assumes that "the brain secretes conscience[o]," or that
"[p] the will is inherent in the substance of the brain,

[k] As we demonstrate to the eye the asymptote of the hyperbola,
it is evident to the senses; as we pursue the demonstration on and
on in thought, the continued approximation of the two lines and
their never meeting, is unimaginable. I remember in my youth,
how to a very clear and powerful mind this fact was of considerable
use, on his way back from unbelief.

[l] Haeckel i. pp 184, 185.   [m] Caussette ii. 357.   [n] Ib. 358.

[o] Cabanis, in his days of unbelief, ap. Caussette ii. 653.

[p] Caussette Ib.

as the power of contraction is in the muscles;" or that "ᴾ it is the aggregate of the brain and the spinal marrow;" or that "ᴾthe brain and the soul are identical, and that man is only a living mechanism, issuing from matter by a developement inherent in its properties;" or that the inextinguishable I, which survives even when (as in some insane�) it seems to be lost, unchanging even while our physical frame is hourly changing, is but a function of that which has no oneness. "The functions of the brain," said an eminent naturalistʳ, "suppose a mutual influence of divisible matter and the indivisible I, which can never be grasped; an impassable hiatus in the system of our ideas, an eternal stumbling-block in all philosophies. Not only do we not understand and never shall understand, how any impressions whatsoever made upon our brain can be perceived by our spirit or produce images therein; but how delicate soever our researches may be, these traces do not exhibit themselves in any way to our eyes, and we are entirely ignorant of their nature."

ꝙ "Dr. Browne, who has done more, I am told, than any other of our day for mental disease, tells me, as the result of the experience of above 30 years; 'my opinion is, that of all mental powers or conditions, the idea of personal identity is but rarely enfeebled, and that it never is extinguished. The Ego and non-Ego may be confused. The Ego however continues to preserve the personality. All the Angels, Devils, Dukes, Lords, Kings, 'gods many,' that I have had under my care, remained what they were, before they became Angels, Dukes, &c., in a sense and even nominally. I have seen a man declaring himself the Saviour, or S. Paul, sign himself *James Thomson*, and attend worship as regularly, as if the notion of Divinity had never entered into his head.'" quoted in Daniel the Prophet pp. 434, 435.

ʳ Cuvier, quoted by Caussette Ib. 654.

It is, again, indifferent to Theology, what part of our wonderful structure physical science decides to be most essential to life. We do not seem to gain much by being told of " [s] a structureless viscid semi-fluid matter common both to plants and animals;" and physicists are not in any way agreed [t] upon " the protoplasmic theory of life." But physical science transgresses its bounds, and invades those of Theology, when it supersedes the action of the soul. We are told that, on this theory [u], " death is death for ever of body mind and soul, for man as for the rest of the animate creation." The soul is no subject of physical science. In the flesh we have no conception of spirit, but we may know certainly, what we cannot picture to ourselves. Physical science can know certainly things in its own province, the material. It cannot establish a negative against the soul or against God.

" It is easily said," writes an eminent natural philosopher [x], " A cell consists of little particles, and these we call Plastidules; but Plastidules consist of Carbon, Hydrogen, Oxygen and Nitrogen, and are provided with a soul of their own : this soul is the product or sum of the forces which the chemical

---

[s] Drysdale, Protoplasmic theory of life p. 18.

[t] Dr. Drysdale, in his ' Protoplasmic Theory of life,' gives and criticises the different theories from 1829 to 1860, and from 1860 onwards.   [u] Drysdale p. 265.

[x] Virchow, Freiheit d. Wissenschaft &c. p. 14. Virchow continues, " this we really cannot require ; on the contrary, my opinion is, that before we stamp such theses as the expression of science, before we say, 'This is modern science,' we must first carry through a whole series of wearisome investigations : we must therefore say to the teachers in schools, 'Do not teach this.' "

atoms possess." "It is possible," he adds, "I cannot determine accurately; it is one of the spots which I cannot yet reach. I feel like a seaman who comes upon a shallow, whose extent he cannot survey: yet I must say that, till the properties of Carbon Hydrogen Oxygen and Nitrogen can be made so clear to me, that I can conceive how a soul can result from the sum of them—till this is done, I cannot yet own that we are entitled to introduce into our teaching a Plastidule-soul, or to require of any educated man to acknowledge it in such wise as scientific truth, as to use it as a logical premiss, and ground upon it his aspect of the world."

Chemical philosophers teach us that nothing in our material world perishes[y]. True; but the inference, that it *could* not be destroyed and therefore must be eternal, does not belong to natural science. *We* cannot destroy it, but our impotency does not prescribe limits to the Omnipotent, or to His creative or preserving Goodness, or His power to annihilate what He has made.

No result of real science ever contradicted Theology; nor do men of real science. One, praised by a pantheist for "his truly scientific method[z],"laid down,

[y] "Natural science teaches that matter is eternal and imperishable, for experience has never shewn us, that even the smallest particle of matter has come into existence or has passed away. Where a natural body seems to disappear, as for example by burning, decaying, evaporation, &c. it merely changes its form, its physical composition or chemical combination." Haeckel, History of creation p. 8. Eng. Tr. Reusch (p. 46) quotes Mohr Geschichte d. Erde, Bonn. 1866.

[z] "Schleiden who founded, thirty years ago, in Jena, a new epoch in Botany by his strictly empirico-philosophical and truly scientific method." Haeckel i. 189.

"[a] The first rule to be observed by the exact sciences is, not to employ themselves about matters which do not fall within the range of their experience, neither affirming nor denying them. But spirit, liberty, God, do not fall under physical observations. How then should the naturalist speak of them? Whether he affirm or deny them, he is equally inconsistent. But if, as a man and not as a naturalist, he speak of these matters, let him remember that second rule of science, not to pronounce a judgement on a matter without thoroughly knowing it."

Natural science is welcome to its conjectures, so long as it does not lay them as the foundation of unbelief in a province not its own. Never probably was any system built upon so many 'perhaps', 'probably,' 'possibly,' 'it may be,' 'it seems to be,' 'most likely,' 'it must be,' 'it requires but a slight stretch of imagination to conceive [b],' as that mythological [c] account of the origin of all which has life, and, at last of ourselves, which is now being every where or widely acknowledged by unscientific minds as if it were axiomatic truth; some of whose adherents claim that it will revolutionise every other science [d].

[a] Schleiden, quoted by Caussette ii. 338.

[b] This lies on the surface of Darwin's books and has been noticed by all critics of Darwinism.

[c] The term 'mythological' is taken from a very thoughtful article in the Rambler (Vol. 2. N. S. p. 363.) on Mr. Darwin's book 'On the origin of species.' The writer fully appreciates " his accumulation and arrangement of scientific facts."

[d] "Manifestly the effect of this conclusion" [the including of man in the supposed genealogy of animals] "is immense, and *no* science will be able to escape from its consequences. Anthropology, or the science of man, and consequently all philosophy, are thereby thoroughly reformed in all their various branches." [Haeckel

A physical philosopher says, "'I ask of any man truly free, of any unprejudiced man, who has occupied himself ever so little with science, ' Is it on such foundations that one would rest any general theory in physics or in chemistry?'" From a limited number of interesting facts has been expanded a theory, unsupported by a single fact. We may think that the 20th century will smile at the credulity of the 19th, unless it sorrows at the boast that "'a personal Creator with His alternate interventions in the progressive changes of organic creation, and especially in the production of our species, is—dismissed." Its transformations, which are confessed, as *we* should confess a truth of revelation, yet undemonstrated, undemonstrable but not needing demonstration, are, if one attempt to picture them to oneself, more akin to the Arabian imaginations than to the calmness of science. Certainly if Almighty God (I venture to utter the irreverence out of reverence to Himself), had had a genealogy of ours, like that which has

Hist. of creation i. pp. 6, 7.] "All the departments of Botany and Zoology, and especially the most important of the latter, Anthropology, become reasonable. The dimming mirage of mythological fiction can no longer exist in the clear sunlight of scientific knowledge." [Ib. p. 11.] Mr Darwin himself says, "In the future I see open fields for far more important researches. Psychology will be securely based on the foundation already well laid by Mr Herbert Spencer, that of the necessary acquirement of each mental power and capacity by gradation. Much light will be thrown on the origin of man and his history." [Darwin, 'Origin of Species,' p. 428.] The German Darwinists hold the same language, as a matter of course.

e De Quatrefages, L'espèce humaine, (Origine des espèces, Hypothèses transformistes) p. 73.

f C. Vogt in Caussette ii. 520.

C

been preserved from Adam, but framed on the assumptions of this mythology [g], and had required us to
believe it as a matter of faith, such a record would have
imposed a trial of faith, greater than the belief of all
the mysteries of faith, and a belief in miracles to
which we have no parallel.

In these days there is a wide-spread and alas! a
growing intolerance of the miraculous. It is thought
to be beyond the powers of evidence, that our Lord
should have recalled the soul of Lazarus into his
body, when it had for four days parted from it. It
was a great miracle, which established in the minds
of the people that Jesus came from God. It *was* a
great miracle: but it was also a great occasion; the
conversion of the world from moral degradation to its
God, from darkness to light. Is it less a miracle that a
certain number of ape-mothers (for there must have
been many to propagate the new race) gave birth to
intelligent beings? Why? but because it pleases
mythology to lay down, that this was the order of
nature; which is dispensing with evidence for the
supernatural by the assumption that it was natural,
A mere begging of the question!

Man, we are told, with all his magnificent intellect, and more magnificent largeness of love, his
powers of beholding God through faith, of aspirations
towards Him, of coyping His Perfections as far as
the finite can receive conceptions of the Infinite, has
risen by an inclined plane of promotion from his fore-
father the ape or some other collateral ancestor among
the vertebrate animals, through which man-like apes,
long since extinct [h], became ape-like men who have

[g] See note A at the end.   [h] Haeckel, ii. 277.

left no trace, for they lived, we are told, so long ago,
"'beyond a doubt more than 20,000, or also *probably*
more than 100,000 years, *perhaps* many hundred
thousands of years." A transformation from the
irrational to the rational, from a thing loathsome
through its habits to a being made in the Image of
God; a transformation which may have taken place
(to take the lowest number,) 20,000 years ago, but
of which there is no evidence, not a trace, is not a
subject of "science" which professes to be "exact."
Yet the animal descent of the human race is said to
be "[k] a necessary and unavoidable inference from
the theory of Descent."

But this is only the beginning of its aggressions.
The theory of our ape-ancestry chose as its sequel,
that man was born in the most degraded state [1], of
which we have any living type, and rose of himself

[i] Haeckel, ii. 297, 298.

[k] Ib. i. 6. Haeckel says, "Darwin himself did not express at first
this most important of all the inferences from his theory. In his
work, 'On the Origin of Species' not a word is found about the
animal descent of man.... It was not till twelve years later, in
his work on 'The Descent of Man, and Selection in Relation to
Sex,' that Darwin openly acknowledged that far-reaching conclusion, and expressly declared his entire agreement with those na-
turalists who had, in the meantime, themselves formed that conclusion."

[1] Apart from this ape-theory, Mr. J. S. Mill so held the original
(it is a contradiction to call it) *debased* state, in which man came
into being, to be unquestioned truth, that it was to him a primary
argument against the benevolence of our Creator, which he thought
could only be explained by His lack of power. The Kantian philosophy, true to man's nature even when it had separated itself
from Christianity, sounded the first recall to the Gospel to many
in Germany, by appealing to the inexorable law, "Thou must."
Mill's statement is given below, note B. at the end.

to the greatest height to which God had restored him,
developing for himself religion and morals. Why?
They did not mean to contradict Holy Scripture.
They forgot it, or ignored it as an antiquated Eastern
imagination, superseded by the advances of natural
science. Probably it did not occur to them, that they
were tacitly ignoring that enquiry, which was the
crux of ancient philosophic thought, 'Whence is
evil?' and tacitly solved it by answering that it was
our apelike propensity, derived to us by "the law of
inheritance."

This inference is arbitrary, whilst it contradicts at
once revealed truth, and, I believe, the history of
mankind. It is the centre of our Christian hope, that
Almighty God, in His love, made us for His love in
His own image and likeness, but that He so prized
the free love of His creature man, that He left him
free, even though he should choose amiss; and when
he had chosen amiss, restored him, if he would. The
separation, if man persevered in it, involved (as we
see) any amount of degradation. You will remember
S. Paul's terrible picture of those who "ᵐ willed not
to retain God in their knowledge." It is a matter of
faith, that God made man perfect "in His own image
and likeness;" but it lies also in our inmost con-
sciousness, that degradation is not our nature, but
our sin.

If it had pleased God in His Omnipotence, that
in those thousands of years ago, an intelligent being
should be born of an unintelligent animal, it would
have been a surpassing miracle, such as He has not
proposed to our faith. It would have been a miracle, akin to the transformations imagined by the

ᵐ Rom. i. 28.

heathen poet. But having assumed thus much, it is arbitrary to limit the change.. If Almighty God had infused into this ape-like creature, the power of giving birth to an intelligent being, on what principle should we have to believe that He limited the gift? The traditions of mankind as to the golden age agree at least so far with the belief in Holy Scripture, that God created man upright and good, not with the later imagination of the Epicurean poet, that man crept out of the ground, "mutum et turpe pecus." Degradation is alas! more natural than moral elevation. We see it, alas, in the midst of our boasted civilisation in our crowded cities. The greater the civilisation, the greater, often, the degradation. The most civilised times of Babylon, Persia, Greece, Rome, were their most degraded. (One might add Nineveh, if its records have been deciphered aright.) If one had to choose one's lot in the midst of degraded humanity, it would be among the Papuans, rather than in the Babylon of old. The terrible picture of S. Paul is but a faint outline of civilised degradation, such as contemporary history records of the civilisation of heathenism. Even in the last century, the Protestant French historian exclaims[n], "It is a cruel miscalculation to have dreamed of the happiness of humanity, and to wake, to find it plunged in blood and tears. But to have dreamed of his virtues and innocence, and fall of a sudden into the evil of unbridled passion, the miscalculation is more cruel still. Our fathers of 1789 were condemned to pass from the perspectives of paradise to scenes of hell. God keep us from forgetting it!"

[n] Guizot, L'Eglise et la Société Chrétiennes, p. 318.

Degradation is everywhere. "Facilis descensus Averni." The way upwards is hard and, for man alone, impossible. "°Man, being in honour and having no understanding, is like the beasts which perish." Had man been born in the degraded state, in which men now picture primæval man, such he would have remained. There is, I believe, in the history of the world no instance of mankind rising unaided.

Its next invasion is of religion and morals. Not to speak of imaginary self-formed religions, if the moral law, instead of being written by the Spirit of God upon our hearts is to be the slow developement of an animal, not we as Christians, but the wiser heathen, who knew of those unwritten and eternal laws [p], would revolt against it. It is to be a developement of the struggle for existence, in which the stronger ever extirpated the weaker, that each was to learn to reverence the other as himself or more than himself, each to love the other, each to be true to the other. "[q]The hiatus"(it has been well said), "cannot be bridged over by any conceivable process of evolution, unless it be evolution by antagonism."

° Ps. xlix. 20.

[p] Sophocles presupposes that they would be recognised by his Athenian audience, in his magnificent appeal of Antigone, " I deemed not that thy proclamations should have such force, that thou, a mortal, shouldest be able to overrule the unwritten and sure laws (ἄγραπτα νόμιμα) of the gods. For not now or yesterday, but ever do they live, and no one knows whence they dawned." (Antig. 452—456.) Demosthenes also presupposes that his hearers would go along with him. " All these things will appear to be so, not only in the laws, but nature herself has defined them by the unwritten laws (τοῖς ἀγράφοις νόμοις), and by the manners of mankind." (de Cor. Opp. 183, i. 4. Dind.)

[q] Nineteenth Century, Sept. 1878 p. 455.

You would be almost startled, were I to ask you, 'Can there be an effect without a cause?' You would, of course, answer me, No. Then, I ask, 'Whence is this power of conceiving absolute Goodness, without beginning, without end, limitless, measureless, all-embracing, the End, Rule, Archetype of all holiness? or of imagining Wisdom, encircling all eternity, receiving into Itself all immensity, drawing to Itself all infinity; the original Impress of all things; in which ignorance can have no place; knowing all things, the present, past, future, the possible, the imaginable, the things which are, the things which are not but could be, pervading all things, but not mixed with any, ever abiding in Its own Beauty, Brilliancy, and Incorruption; the Essential Source of all beauty and purity; Holy in Itself of Its own Essence by a true'self-dependent Holiness?' These conceptions are not the soul's inheritance from any ape-like ancestors, nor are they any natural insensible variations from them. Yet these, we are told, are the two laws of our descent.

The brute-creation, most familiar with man, learn from him something of right and wrong. Whence did man learn it? We know that we have our sense of right, not from any agreement among our kind, not from utility, but because it is written on the heart of every individual, from which it has not been effaced. Whence did Regulus learn his self-sacrificing truthfulness, or Scipio his self-denying purity? I might ask, thus far, Whence had the tent-maker that zeal, whereby he sped from East to West and endured those daily deaths, for the well-being of his fellow-men? Whence had he that love for his unseen Lord, whereby he counted all things loss, so that he might

win Christ? Whence—one may dare to utter blasphemy to save others from conscious blasphemy,—
Whence were the Soul and Mind of Christ? Were
these too derived from the pithecoids?

Yes, this is the central evil, that to so many physical philosophers of the present day it may be said,
as the Baptist said to the Jews, "There standeth
One among you, Whom ye know not;" as they themselves said afterwards, " ʳAs for this Man, we know
not whence He is." Predicted of beforehand by a
long chain of prophets, as One Who should come to
save our human race, believed in, hoped in, before He
came; proclaimed as the "ˢMighty God, the Prince of
peace, of the increase of Whose government and peace
there shall be no end," but as "ᵗthe Man of sorrows,
and the friend of grief," He came to suffer here and
be crucified; to reign after death. Cradled in a
manger, not having where to lay His Head, followed
by an unlettered multitude, despised by the wise of
His people; He was mocked, scourged, crucified, and
reigned.

His Death was the dawn of His reign. The blood-
stained Robber who died the same death as Himself,
was the last conquest of His life; the Centurion at
the foot of His Cross was the first victory of His
Death. A few days more and His enemies up-
braided His disciples, "ᵘYe have filled Jerusalem
with your doctrine."

Human empires grow, swell, vanish: the more
they swell, the sooner they vanish. Jesus said,
" ˣIf I be lifted up from the earth, I shall draw all

ʳ S. John ix. 29.   ˢ Isa. ix. 6.   ᵗ Ib. liii. 3.
       ᵘ Acts v. 28.   ˣ S. John xii. 32.

men unto Me," and the gibbet of slaves, the exe-
cration of the world, became the sceptre of His
power. His empire reaches from East to West, from
pole to pole; by the foolishness of the Cross He
has taken captive human intellect as well as human weakness. His reign is not measured by the
hundreds of millions who bear His Name, but by
the units in those hundreds of millions, who, one
by one, love Him with an absorbing, self-sacrificing
love. For He reigns by a mightier power than Wisdom or Strength, by His indivisible individual Love.
The African savage melts at the sight of the symbol
of His Passion. He reigns, not by that Infinite love
alone, which He shewed 1800 years ago on Calvary;
but by that individual love, wherewith He loves
every human heart which He has made. "The Voice
of Jesus" still "sounds o'er land and sea," and in the
depth of the aching heart, He still speaks aloud from
His Throne in glory, "[y] Come unto Me, all ye that are
weary and heavy laden, and I will give you rest;" and
to those, who, after their wanderings, come to Him,
He gives it. His Cross is still the magnet of His
love. "[z] We love Him, because He first loved us."
Nothing is too degraded, nothing too sunk in the mire
of sin, which His Divine Wisdom will not seek out
diligently until He find it, and finding, He rejoiceth.
The reality of the elevation of our degraded humanity
is at once an evidence of its Divine Original; of His
Divine power, Who can raise it; of His Divine Love
Who loves it. The resurrection of each single soul
is a greater miracle than the resurrection of Lazarus.
True, that as was foretold of Him, He still "[a] reigns

[y] S. Matt. xi. 28.   [z] 1 S. John iv. 19.   [a] Ps. cx. 1.

in the midst of His enemies:" but He still loves His
enemies: He loves those who hate Him; He still in-
tercedes for them: He still longs that they should
love Him: He will still win them to His love, if they
leave any avenue of their heart, where He can enter
in; if they shut Him not out to the last.   Whether
you yet love Him, or whether any of you has, alas!
ceased to love Him, or whether your love has been
chilled in the midst of the eagerness of an intellectual
feverishness, He still loves you with that Infinite
Love, which He Himself Is.   Yield thyself to His
love, and no perplexities of intellect will ever over-
power thee; for "the heart has its own convictions[b],"
which are immoveable because they are from God.
"[c]I know in Whom I have believed," said one, who
knew what it was to love Jesus, whom Jesus had won
by His love to His love: "[d]I am persuaded, that
neither death, nor life, nor angels, nor principalities,
nor powers, nor things present, nor things to come,
nor height, nor depth, nor any other creature, shall
be able to separate us from the love of God, which
is in Christ Jesus our Lord."

[b] "Le cœur a ses raisons, que la raison ne connoit pas : on le sent
en mille manières."   Pascal, Pensées, P. ii. Art. xvii. n. 5.
     [c] 2 Tim. i. 12.   [d] Rom. viii. 38, 39.

Haeckel's pedigree runs thus;

1) Inorganic combinations of carbon oxygen hydrogen nitrogen spontaneously generated living creatures, ' organisms without organs,' i. e., simple homogeneous, structureless, formless, little lumps of albuminous matter, like the still living Protamœba primitiva; "of which large numbers still exist." [The existence of these is, I believe, given up.] Haeckel himself declares The *assumption* of this stage is *necessary* for most important '*general reasons*' [ii. pp. 278, 279.] The 'general reasons' being the exclusion of a Creator.

2) These generated "Amœbæ" or "single-celled organisms;"

3) The "Amœbæ" generated "Synamœbæ" or community of Amœbæ;

4) The "Synamœbæ" generated the "Ciliated larvæ" [this stage we are told, has been lost, but 'must have existed'];

5) The "Ciliated larvæ" generated "Gastræada or primæval stomach-animals" [which we are told again 'must have existed' and 'must also have included the ancestors of man'];

6) The "Gastræada" generated "low worms, closely allied to the Gliding-worms;"

7) The "Gliding-worms" generated, 'at least one connecting intermediate stage, in the wide gap between the "Gliding worms" and the Tunicata, which we may comprise as "Soft-worms;"' ['of which no fossil remains exist, owing to the soft nature of their bodies'];

8) "The Soft-worms" generated the "Sack-worms;"

9) The "Sack-worms" generated the "Skull-less animals" [of which the Amphioxus is the nearest representative] who is, we are told, 'flesh of our flesh and blood of our blood' [Haeckel Anthropogenie p. 337] 'who is also, next to man, the most interesting of all the vertebrate animals' [Ib. pp. 176, 298.]; 'who is to be contemplated with especial reverence as that worthy beast which, among all living beasts, can alone give us an approximate idea of our eldest Silurian vertebrate ancestors' [Haeckel, quoted by Reusch p. 420]; 'unfortunately' however 'they could leave no

fossil remains, on account of the absence of any solid skeleton'
[Haeckel Hist. of creation ii. 199];

10) "The Skull-less animals" generated "the single-nostriled
animals;"

11) The "single-nostriled animals" generated "the primæval
fish;"

12) "The primæval fish" generated "the mud-fish;"

13) "The mud-fish" generated "the gilled amphibians;"

14) "The gilled amphibians" generated "the tailed amphibians;" [They "*originated* out of the gilled Amphibians by *accus-
toming themselves* in early life to breathe only through gills and
later in life only through lungs"];

15) The 'unknown' "*tailed amphibians" generated "primæval
amniota" [two stages, whose existence is only proved by their being "necessary intermediate links"];

16) The "primæval amniota" generated the "primary mammals" 'long since extinct and unknown' [in whom we are told
' we find ourselves more at home with our ancestors'];

17) The "primary mammals" generated "the marsupials;"

18) "The marsupials" generated "the Semi-apes;"

19) The "Semi-apes" generated "the narrow-nosed tailed
apes;"['closely related by blood to man'] 'probably as early as the
older Tertiary period;'

20) "The narrow-nosed tailed Apes" generated "the man-like
apes," anthropoides, as now existing [of whom however 'there
do not exist direct human ancestors, but they certainly existed
among the unknown extinct Human Apes of the Miocene period'];

21) "The man-like apes" generated "the ape-like speechless
men" ['whose existence is arrived at by an enquiring mind from
comparative philology, or the history of the developement of language in every child and in every nation'];

22) "The speechless ape-like men" generated "Genuine Men,
' probably about the diluvial period.' [Haeckel's History of creation, ii. pp. 278—295.]

Mr. Darwin, in his Descent of man, expresses his admiration
of the ingenuity shewn in Haeckel's genealogy, but says, on the
authority of " a most capable judge," that "no true bird or reptile
intervened in the direct line of descent;" he recognizes however,

---

* 'Our most ancient ancestors of the class of amphibia.' Haeckel ii. p. 288.

I.) ancestors as simply or even still more simply organs than the lancelet or amphioxus; "some amphibian-like creature, and this again from some fish-like animal, more like the existing marine Ascidians than any other known form" (p. 609); and [nearer to man],

II.) 1 Monotremata, 2 Marsupials, 3 Lemuridæ, 4 Simiadæ, 5 Catarrhine monkeys. The conclusion, he thinks, may revolt our *pride;* but we must conclude that our early progenitors would have been properly thus designated. "But," he adds, "we must not fall into the error of supposing that the early progenitors of the whole Simian stock, including man, was identical with *or even closely resembled* any existing ape or monkey." [Descent of man, p. 155.] But if they did not *resemble* any existing ape or monkey, on what ground is it assumed that they were apes or monkeys at all?

Rolle, his translator, recognized the genealogy as far back as fishes and reptiles. [Der Mensch, seine Abstammung &c. p. 108.]

De Quatrefages objects to the ape-ancestry of man on Darwinian principles:

'In Darwin's theory, transformations do not take place by chance or any how—An organism, once modified in a certain way, may undergo secondary tertiary &c. transformations, but it will still always retain the impress of the original type.—Consequently, two creatures, belonging to two distinct types, may go back to a common ancestor, which was not yet distinctly characterised, but they cannot descend, the one from the other. But man and the apes in general present a very marked contrast of type.

'Their organs, as we have already said, correspond almost exactly with each other. But these organs are disposed on a very different plan. In man, they are co-ordinated in such wise that he is of necessity, *a walker:* in the monkeys, in such wise, that they are, not less imperiously, *climbers.*

'This is an anatomical and mechanical distinction already established as to the inferior apes by the labours of Vicq-d'Azyr, Lawrence, Serres &c. The studies of Duvernoy on the Gorilla, of Gratiolet and of M. Alix on the Chimpanzee, have put beyond question, that all anthropomorphous apes exhibited in all points the same fundamental character.

'It is enough to cast an eye at the drawing, where Huxley has placed side by side a human skeleton and the skeletons of the highest apes, to be convinced that this is indeed so.

' The result of these facts, in view of the logical application of the *law of permanent characterisation*, is, that man cannot descend from an ancestor already characterised as an ape, whether a catarrhine without a tail or a catarrhine with a tail. A walking animal cannot descend from a climbing animal. Vogt understood· this very well. Though placing man in the number of the *primates*, he hesitates not to declare that the lower apes have passed the *jalon* (common ancestry), from which the various types of this family have diverged.

'The origin of man must then be thrown back beyond the last ape, if one of the laws, most imperiously requisite for the doctrinal edifice of Darwinism, is to be maintained. One comes thus to Haeckel's *prosimians*, the loris, indris &c.

'But these animals are also climbers. We must then seek still further for our first direct ancestor. But for that, the genealogy traced by Haeckel gives us the marsupials.

'The Kangaroo, it will be owned, is a good way off from man. But neither living nature nor the fossil-remains of extinct animals present the intermediate types which ought at least to connect them.

' This difficulty did not trouble Darwin ; we know that he meets it by saying that the absence of information on the like questions is a proof in his favour : Haeckel without doubt will be as little embarrassed. We have seen him admit an equally theoretical ' pithecoid man ' and this is not the only time that he uses this process in framing his genealogical table. Amongst others he says of the Sozures (14th stage), ' amphibians,' equally unknown to science : "The proof of their existence lies in the necessity for this intermediate link between the 13th and 15th stage."

'Well ! it is now demonstrated, on the part of Darwinism itself, that the ancestry of man must be sent back beyond the 18th stage. As it consequently becomes necessary to fill up the gap from the marsupials to man, will Haeckel admit four unknown intermediate groups instead of one ? Will he thus complete his genealogy ? It is not for me to say.' [De Quatrefages, pp. 78, 79.]

There is, indeed, nothing new in the mythology itself. 1. De Maillet thought it nothing stranger that a fish should be changed

into a bird, than that a chrysalis should become a butterfly. Flying fish might, he thought, have and did become birds, being out of
their element, under the influence of the air; as Mr. Darwin says
that " it is conceivable that flying fish might have been modified
into perfectly winged animals." [Origin of Species p. 140. ed. 6.]
He originated the theory of the transmutation of species and in lieu
of facts appealed to his personal conviction and possibilities. [De
Quatrefages, C. Darwin et ses précurseurs Français pp. 19—32.]
He too thought that we should find in the sea our first ancestors.
[Ib. p. 29.] 2. Robinet's fancies were chiefly negative; he held
that genera and species were but illusions, that nature made no
leaps, that inanimate nature was really animate; that all is progressive from minerals to vegetables, thence to animals, thence to
man, that all beings must have come from some prototype, and that
force might gradually free itself from all material and begin a
new world.' He lived to retract. [DeQ.ib. pp. 33—39.] 3. Buffon
united the two ideas of species and race, and first laid the foundation
of the theory of the influence of surroundings (du milieu), and
called attention to the influence of domestication. [Ib. pp. 40—42.
His theory was scientific, not transformist]. 4. Lamarck began with
spontaneous generation and, thence, transmitted growth. He supposed that God created forces and matter. ' Nature is in some way
an intermedium between God and the parts of the physical universe
for the execution of His will.' [Hist. nat. d. animaux sans vertèbres,
Introd.] He introduced a belief in progressive and retrogressive
transmutation, the length of time required; he ascribed the formation of each new organ to some new want of the animal, and
a consequent new movement. Hence in successive generations
snails gained their feelers; ant-eaters and wood-peckers their long
tongues; ruminants, their horns by fighting with their foreheads;
kangaroos, their large hinder limbs and tail and small fore-paws,
to leap the better; seals, on land, became carnivora and acquired
claws; lamantine became ruminating animals provided with hoofs;
aquatic mammifera lost their hind limbs. Serpents prolonged
their bodies and lost their paws; birds became web-footed, or
long-legged, or long-necked; by efforts to browse on trees the
giraffe had at once its neck and fore-legs lengthened (in all the
individuals of the race); beasts of prey gained their claws, to
tear; the power of drawing them in, to walk; serpents and fish
changed the position of their eyes. He made two genealogies.

The latest was, I.) Inarticulate animals. 1 Infusories. 2 Polypi. 3 Ascidians. 4 Acephali. 5 Molluscs. II.) Articulati. 1 Worms. 2 Epizoa. 3 Insects. (4a Arachnidæ) 4 Crustaceans. 5 Cirripedes. [Philosophie Zoologique c. 7. Additions T. ii.]

5. Geoffry Saint Hilaire thought that the 'surroundings' were the single cause of the changes of organisms, especially the chemical composition of the atmosphere. " Every thing is regulated by intervention of respiration." He would not admit *one* prototype : he denied insensible changes, but thought that a reptile might become a bird. [Ib. pp. 60—67.] Darwin too thinks that a well developed tail of an aquatic animal might come to be worked in for all sorts of purposes, as a fly-flapper, an organ of prehension, or an aid in turning, though slight in dogs. [Orig. of Species p. 357].

6. The son, Isidore Geoffry S. Hilaire was no transformist. [De Q. ib. pp. 67—69.]

7. The eminent botanist, M. Naudin, recognised in existing living things, a certain *plasticity*, an aptitude to undergo modification, according to the difference of their surroundings, limited by the law of inheritance, itself limited by *finality*, ' a mysterious undetermined power, which is to some fatalism, to others a providential Will, whose unceasing action determines, at all epochs of the existence of the world, the form, volume, and duration of each, according to its destination in the order of things, of which it forms a part.' He assumed a ' number of primordial types, relatively small, from which nature successively and at different epochs produced all the vegetable and animal species which people the globe.' Whether this ' natural selection' implies 'an intelligent Nature, acting to a determined end and producing by a rational selection, or whether natural selection be the necessary result of anterior facts, M. Naudin does not say.' [Ib. pp. 70 —74.]

Mr. Darwin, who adds to 'natural selection' the struggle for existence, (which, he says, was an application of the theory of Malthus to animals) leaves it equally undetermined whether by ' natural selection' he means an Agent, the Superintending Providence of Almighty God ; his personification of it makes one hope that he does; only he tells us that he does *not* mean His Creative Power. This denial of Creative agency much embarrasses his theory of gradual modifications of complex structures.

He himself acknowledges, " If it could be demonstrated that any complex organ existed which could not possibly have been formed by numerous successive slight modifications, my theory would absolutely break down." [Origin of Species, p. 146. ed. 6.]

To speak of the formation of the eye only, Reusch says, [Bibel und Natur, p. 386.] "The discussion of this point is one of the best parts in Frohschammer's criticism on Darwinism. He says very aptly, 'So therefore out of imperfect eyes *without* crystal lenses and all besides, eyes *with* crystal lenses and horny surface are to be formed by natural selection. That could only happen, either if, in that most imperfect eye, this perfect one were already laid as in a seed, which only needs developement; but this would imply an inner principle of developement, and the external principle of developement by natural selection, assumed by Darwin, would be superfluous, or at least, no longer the primary and only principle; or, if the capacity for further improvement or for adding to the crystal lens did not yet exist in that most imperfect eye, then its formation even in its very earliest beginnings could only have been either through *generatio æquivoca*, or through accident, or through a distinctly divine creative agency. As Darwin accepts nothing of all this, the matter remains unexplained; i.e. the possibility of the transformation is not shewn, and the difficulty is not therefore solved. Darwin indeed likens the perfect eye to the telescope, and the action of " natural selection" in relation to the perfecting of the eye, to the exertions of human intelligence in the improvement and perfecting of the telescope. But this is certainly wrong; for unconscious nature can no more imitate or exercise the activity of the optician carried on upon a definite plan, than it can imitate or replace the activity of the artist, e.g. of the painter or the clockmaker. The material requirements for works of art certainly all exist in nature; but nevertheless, no one could say, that nature is able of itself to produce a painting or a clock. Darwin on this point falls into a formal Personification of natural selection, in order to keep up his limping explanation of the origin of the perfected eye. Natural selection is to 'observe minutely,' and 'select carefully,' and 'with unerring tact discover each improvement for further perfecting.' Were that to be understood literally, Darwin would himself thereby introduce into nature a power acting according to design, which would make all his other attempts at explanation superfluous. But any how, according to

D

Darwin's intention, it is only to be understood figuratively, and then such expressions are perfectly inadmissible. "Natural selection," as the complex of merely operating causes, cannot observe, select, and proceed on a definite plan, but must take every thing as it comes, and can only use and retain favourable circumstances or alterations; or more justly expressed, these changes, when they once exist, maintain themselves, because they exist. Natural selection therefore cannot strive for more perfect eyes, but can only preserve them, and use them, when they exist and therefore have in some way originated. The most perfect eyes cannot be explained by numerous slight successive modifications: for they are distinguished from the imperfect eyes by substantially *new* parts which cannot issue in continual developement out of the former, unless they are already laid up in them from the beginning on a regular plan; in which case they could only have arisen through a sudden spring, and so through an incomprehensible, mysterious occurrence, not through natural selection.' [Das Christenthum p. 517.]" Reusch also quotes Pfaff, Die neuesten Forschungen, p. 102. See also St. George Mivart, On the genesis of species, pp. 57—61. And Prof. Pritchard, Hulsean Lectures, Appendix Note A pp. 122—128.

NOTE B. p. 35.

Mr. Mill's picture is this, "If the motive of the Deity for creating sentient beings was the happiness of the beings He created, His purpose, in our corner of the universe at least, must be pronounced, taking past ages and all countries and races into account, to have been thus far an ignominious failure; and if God had no purpose but our happiness and that of other creatures, it is not credible that He would have called them into existence with the prospect of being so completely baffled. If man had not the power, by the exercise of his own energies for the improvement both of himself and of his outward circumstances, to do for himself and other creatures vastly more than God had in the first instance done, the Being Who called him into existence would deserve something very different from thanks at his hands. Of course it may be said that this very capacity of improving himself and the world was given to him by God, and that the change, which he will be thereby enabled ultimately to effect in human existence, will be worth purchasing by the sufferings and wasted lives of entire geological periods. This may be so; but to suppose that God could not have given him these blessings at a less frightful cost, is to make a very strange supposition concerning the Deity. It is to suppose that God could not, in the first instance, create anything better than a Bosjesman or an Andaman islander, or something still lower; and yet was able to endow the Bosjesman or the Andaman islander with the power of raising himself into a Newton or a Fenelon. We certainly do not know the nature of the barriers which limit the divine Omnipotence; but it is a very odd notion of them, that they enable the Deity to confer on an almost bestial creature the power of producing by a succession of efforts what God Himself had no other means of creating." [Three Essays on Religion: Theism, Attributes, pp. 192, 193; Mr. Mill repeats this in his Essay on Nature, pp. 42, 43.]

Educated as an Atheist and emerging thence to think that it was probable that there was a God of limited power, and, if so, that "there is nothing so inherently impossible or absolutely incredible in this supposition as to preclude any one from hoping that it may perhaps be true, that Jesus, as he openly proclaimed, came from God," Mr. Mill had no notion that this picture of God's dealings with man has no other basis than the traditional unbelief of his surroundings. He first ignorantly misrepresents Almighty God, contrary to His own revelation of Himself, and then founds his accusations on these imaginings of his school. As an Atheist, he could, of course, have no idea of sin, or of God's dealings with a sinful world, or a world, in which His rational creatures would, to such an extent, need corrective discipline; still less, of course, that that discipline would be healing to the soul.

I have been asked, in the name of some young members of the University who heard this sermon, whether I account the *animal* derivation of the *body* of man to be a theory contradictory to Revelation, and should, on theological grounds, hold it to be impossible that science could establish it. I would, in answer, recall the distinction between the scientific and what has been called "the mythological" or transformist part of Mr. Darwin's theory.

The question as to "species," of what variations the animal world is capable, whether the species be more or fewer, whether accidental variations may become hereditary, whether the "struggle for existence" may have occasioned animals which once existed to disappear, whether e. g. the animals, ranged under the tribes of felis, canis[1], bos, ovis, were each originally variations of some common progenitor, and the like, naturally fall under the province of science. In all these questions Mr. Darwin's careful observations gained for him a deserved approbation and confidence.

These questions have no bearing whatever upon Theology. Professor Reusch says, "I should not be at all concerned about Vogt's statement in 1863 (when he had other views than now), to the effect that he must decline the last results of the Darwinian system, but that, in regard to the more nearly-related types, he could declare himself an adherent of it. With this restriction, I could myself become a Darwinian without ceasing to be a Theologian who believes in the Bible: a relationship of race between more nearly related types of the animal and vegetable kingdom, even when one extends the relationship very far, has theologically nothing which one need apprehend." [Bibel und Natur, p. 373.]

Darwin's scientific explanations, all his facts relate only to a wide extension of species; in his transformist theories alone, he appeals to the "possible" and his own "personal convictions." But possibilities are no basis for science. "Modern science is more exacting. Above all, as M. Chevreul has well shewn, it appeals to observation and experience; it accepts as proofs only well-defined facts, the exactness of which have been established by a solid verification. Doubtless, it does not interdict logical induction, conducting the intelligence somewhat beyond the positive and immediate consequences of the phenomena established; but it denies the right of substituting single *conjectures* for facts, and making them the ground of consequences. Much less, can it ascribe any authority whatever to 'possibilities.'" (De Quatrefages, C. Darwin &c. p. 152.)

"Doubtless" says the same writer, "every species is subject to variations; doubtless in presence of facts which accumulate day by day, one must recognise that the limits of variation are much wider

[1] De Quatrefages thinks that all dogs (of which 180 perfectly distinct races were collected at a Paris exhibition) are from one stock; contrary to Darwin, (Origin of Species p. 15.) De Q., Darwin &c. P. ii. c. 6. p. 276.

than some great masters of science, e. g. Cuvier, have admitted. But nothing hitherto shews that they are transmutable. Every where around us races spring up, develope and disappear; no where has it appeared that one species is engendered by another species, that a higher type has come out of a lower."

Unhappily, on his scientific investigations Darwin grafted a theory which belonged to theology, not to natural science. In geological remains, there has been observed a gradation from the more imperfect to the more advanced. This might obviously have been through the continued action of the Creator and, down to Lamarck and Mr. Darwin, was held by scientific men also to have been so. No one doubted it, who believed in creation at all. We were not there, and as we cannot understand why God created at all, so neither can we tell what end He had in creating anything which He did create.

We know that God created orders of beings of immense intelligence, of whose numbers we know nothing. The number of stars, which the increased power of our telescopes have discovered to astronomers, involves a creation of fixed stars or suns, which, Sir J. Herschell told us, " may be really infinite, in the only sense in which we can assign a meaning to the word " (i. e. as to things created). [Outlines of Astronomy, n. 771.] " The united lustre of myriads of stars is perceptible only in powerful telescopes as a feeble nebulous gleam." The nearest fixed star is, according to the same astronomer, about 20 billions of miles from this earth. [Some extracts, which are in so many books, I have put together in notes on my Sermon on the Ascension, Parochial Sermons, Vol. ii. pp. 222—225.] In this immensity of creation, it seems to me an improbable assumption, that all the creations in this our planet were completed at once. It was chiefly in order to escape the belief that there were successive creations, [or, in our language, a continuous creation] that the theory of evolution was invented. Mr. Darwin urges this in self-defence against critics of his book. " I may be permitted to say, as some excuse, that I had two distinct objects in view; firstly, to shew that species had not been separately created, and secondly, that natural selection had been the chief agent of change, though largely aided by the inherited effects of habit, and slightly by the direct action of the surrounding conditions. I was not, however, *able to annul the influence of my former belief, then almost universal, that each species had been purposely created*; and this led to my tacit assumption, that any detail of structure, excepting rudiments, was of some special, though unrecognised, service. Any one, with this assumption in his mind, would naturally extend too far the action of natural selection, either during past or present times. Some of those who admit the principle of evolution, but reject natural selection, seem to forget, when criticising my book, that I had the above two objects in view; hence, if I have erred in giving to natural selection great power, which I am very far from admitting, or in having exaggerated its power, which is in itself probable, *I have at least, as I hope, done good service in aiding to overthrow the dogma of separate creations.*" [Darwin, the Descent of man, P. 1. c. 2. p. 61.]

It was then, so far, with a quasi-Theological, not with a scientific object, that he wrote his book. He wished " to overthrow the dogma of separate creations." Why? With the all-but-infinity of creation, which the telescope unfolds, what are we, that we should object to any mode of creation, as unbefitting our Creator? A result, which is arrived at under a bias, lies under a suspicion as to its validity. People catch at what seems to them evidence, on what seems to them previous probability. The reproach is cast upon Theologians; it is not likely to belong to them alone. To myself, when Mr. Darwin's book first appeared, it seemed (as I designated it) "a transparent paralogism of 'non causa pro causa.'" [Univ. Sermons, 1859 —1872. p. 42.] I do not myself believe that it *can* become scientific truth; for the period, to which it relates, is so remote as to exclude the *knowledge* of facts which would determine it. Even granted, that intermediate types (the absence of which is so strongly urged against Mr. Darwin's theory, a lacuna which he himself in a degree feels, although he ascribes it to the imperfections of our geological records)—even granted that intermediate types had existed, the question, whether the one creature were the offspring of the other, or whether each was directly created by God, is one which there would be no evidence to determine. There is absolutely no evidence now, that there ever were such transformations, as that "marsupials generated semi-apes." For thousands of years (or tens of thousands according to these theorists) there is no trace of any such change. The only presumption that it ever was, the only evidence which science would admit in any other case, would be, its taking place *now, when science could examine the evidence for the alleged facts.* Nature remains the same; its laws are the same. Why, if they were not regulated by the will of its Creator, was it once so prolific in forming new classes of animals, and now is still?

Haeckelians have felt this difficulty as to the production of the first matter, out of which the successive developements, they think, may have arisen. In so many words, they say, in fact, " we do not know."

" At the present time," says Burmeister, " when every where there are creatures enough capable of reproduction, there is in truth no need for the formation of any new creation out of aboriginal matter. Also, perhaps, there is lacking the material basis for it, whence they could be formed, since most by far of the organic substance of the present is to be found already in living organisms, and there appears to be no store, whence new individuals could originate, in any other way than through generation. But in the aboriginal time of organisation, all this was different, and therefore also the course of formation was different." [Gesch. d. Schopfung, p. 287, in Reusch, p. 340.]

Haeckel argues from our ignorance, ' How can we know that in remote primæval times there did not exist conditions quite different from those at present obtaining, and which may have rendered spontaneous generation possible? . . . . At the time when, after the origin of water in a liquid state on the cooled crust of the earth, organisms were first formed by spontaneous generation, those innumerable quantities of Carbon existed in a totally different form, *probably* for the most part dispersed in the atmosphere in the shape of carbonic acid. The whole composition of the atmosphere *was therefore* extremely different from the present. Further, as may be inferred upon chemical, physical, and geological grounds, the density and the electrical conditions of the atmosphere were quite different. In like manner the chemical and physical nature of the primæval ocean, which then continuously covered the whole surface of the earth as an uninterrupted watery sheet, was quite peculiar. The temperature, the density, the amount of salt &c., *must* have been very different from those of the present ocean. In any case therefore, even *if we do not know anything more about it, there remains to us the supposition, which can at least not be disputed, that, at that time, under conditions quite different from those of to-day, a spontaneous generation, which now is perhaps no longer possible, may have perhaps taken place.*' [Hist. of creation, T. i. pp. 341, 342.]

Granted that the possibility may not be disputable, an undisputed *possibility* is not a substitute for certain facts in an exact science. Granting (for the moment) the *possibility* that ' a marsupial may

generate an ape,' this does not establish, as a matter of exact science,
that it ever did ; and the absence of any like transformation in any
historical period, at least establishes a probability against such changes
altogether. Any how they are no matter of 'science,' i. e. certain
knowledge founded on certain facts.

The transformation-theory of Darwin is quite apart from the
" survival of the strongest in the battle for life." This struggle
would be between animals of the same general habits of life. It
is in keeping, that rats, leeches, cock-roaches, bees, swallows,
thrushes, should have supplanted others of their own kind. [Darwin's
Origin &c. p. 59. ed. 6.] But our supposed progenitors survive
still. Kangaroos and apes still exist. The transformation-theory was
a special object of Darwin's interest, he tells us, because it dispensed
with the intervention of a personal Creator. Darwin's German
translator noted the inconsistency of assuming for once a First Cause,
and then denying His interference ever after. " A personal act of
creation is still required for Darwin's first organic being, and if it is
requisite once, then it appears to us an utter matter of indifference,
whether the first act of creation occupied itself with one or with
ten or with a hundred thousand species." [Bronn, p. 516, quoted
by Reusch, p. 351.] De Quatrefages insists on it as " an absolutely
arbitrary hypothesis, which was against all the analogies drawn from
the history of all the branches of human knowledge." (Darwin et ses
précurseurs, p. 204.)

Darwinism was acceptable to German atheists, because, with
that one exception, it removed God out of sight. " As I observed
before," says C. Vogt, " this Creator, who from time to time
changed the furnishing of his earth, and created a new one after
he had annihilated the old, would never get into my head.—It
is not strange, that the view of Darwin met with the most vehe-
ment contradiction.—Its consequences are unquestionably frightful for a certain direction of mind. There is no question that
Darwin's theory, without any ceremony, turns out of doors a Personal Creator and his interferences in the change of the creation,
and the creation of species, in that it does not leave the very least
room for the working of such a being." [Vorlesungen, ii. pp. 259, 260.]
A graver writer says, " This is the great attractiveness of this
theory. It points out to materialism a possibility of referring
the origin and continued existence of all living beings to an ac-

cidental coincidence of external physical and chemical processes. Darwin has brought the goal, at which Materialism drives with all its might, so invitingly near." [Pfaff, die neuesten Forschungen, p. 107.] Rolle says, " After the advance of science had long stood in awe before this last bulwark of the theory of creation, it was reserved to Darwin &c." [Der Mensch, &c. p. 64.]

" No where was the theory better received than in Germany; it suits better than any other its Pantheistic aspirations." [Dumont, Haeckel, c. 3.]

It is, of course, an invasion of a foreign province, when Darwinism speculates upon man's developement of religion and morals. For physical science has obviously nothing to do with either. It is a strange petitio principii to assume, that man *must* have come into the world in the lowest intellectual and moral condition, in which he can exist, and not cease to be man. It is no honour to the philosophic character of the Nineteenth century, that it can assume this primæval condition of man, as an unquestionable fact. It may be natural for one born of a pithecoid, as far as one speaks of what would be natural to a creature, which is itself a myth. But such assumptions are not the bases of solid science.

Darwinism, then, is in an inconsistent position. It is not Atheistic in itself; it cannot be so, except by the further assumption of the eternity of matter and spontaneous generation. But it is inconsistent, in its belief in a Creator Who is to be eliminated from all interference with the works which He has made. This inconsistency is aggravated by the assumption of almost boundless time, with which the mind can as little " grapple, as with the idea of eternity." [Origin of Species, p. 269 ed. 6.]

A First Cause, which is introduced as a ' Deus ex machinâ,' to save us from the conception of the eternity of matter, but who, after the creation, looked on unconcerned upon the results of his act upon his creatures, would be an Epicurean god, whose being would be inconsistent not only with God's revelation of Himself, but with any conceptions of an intelligent Theism.

But this belief Darwin tells us, it was his object to establish. It was the essence of Darwinism.

The belief then that an animal, in its physical birth, was endowed by Almighty God, not with reason only, but with a soul; that the being so produced had a full power of understanding good and evil, and choosing between them : that Almighty God placed before the creature, thus made, the choice, and that it deliberately chose to disobey its God; this would be completely at variance with the first principles of Darwinism. To what end to theorise about gradual developement, the only interest of which is to exclude a Creator, if it is to end in such an abrupt conclusion as this?

Mr. Darwin himself says 'it is impossible to fix any definite point when the term *man* ought to be used in the insensible graduation from some ape-like creature.' [Descent of man, p. 180.]

My answer then to my young friends is this;

It lies as the basis of our faith, that man was created in the perfection of our nature, endowed with supernatural grace, with a full freedom of choice, such as man, until restored by Christ, has not had since. If science could prove, that our race was born of an ape-mother, one should be forced to the belief, that God took away at once all the propensities which it had by the 'law of inheritance,' and gave it a soul, made in His own likeness. But since all science must rest on a basis of certain ascertained facts, and the question as to the 'mythological' part of Darwinism relates altogether not to facts, but to the *mode* of the production of creatures so many thousands of years ago, of which *mode* of production, there is absolutely no record; since, moreover, there can be, in the future, no such facts, unless hereafter Almighty God should endow an animal with a power of production of such sort as Mr. Darwin assumes, that 'mythological' part of Darwinism, not resting on *certain* facts, cannot become matter of science, and we need not entertain the question, whether theology would repudiate it, if it were science; since (so long as it shall exist) it must continue to be only a theory held, or not denied, by some scientific men, and cannot become a science.

A thoughtful writer says, "The condemnation of Darwinism is not its framing hypotheses, but that these hypotheses are bad. No science can do without hypotheses. Good hypotheses can clearly be of great use to any science, but hypotheses are only admissible to explain established facts. Hypotheses are inadmissible, which not only require for their support the assumption of new hypotheses, but also require facts which are altogether unproven. But the Darwinian doctrine eminently requires such assumptions, and therefore it is scientifically a bad and inadmissible theory." [I. B. Meyer, Philos. Zeitfragen, p. 103. quoted by Reusch, p. 383.]

PRINTED BY THE DEVONPORT SOCIETY OF THE HOLY TRINITY, HOLY ROOD, OXFORD.

www.ingramcontent.com/pod-product-compliance
Lightning Source LLC
Chambersburg PA
CBHW031755090426
42739CB00008B/1022